Encounters wi..

The Epistle of Paul
the Apostle
to the HEBREWS

Encounters with God

The Epistle of Paul the Apostle to the HEBREWS

CONTENTS

An Introduction to the Epistle to the Hebrews

This study guide covers the epistle to the Hebrews. In a number of ways, Hebrews is the mystery book of the New Testament. We are not certain of the author, nor the intended recipients. Hebrews does not follow a format identical to that of any other book: it begins as a carefully composed, formal treatise, proceeds as a sermon, and concludes as a letter.

What we do know is that Hebrews includes all the major themes of the Gospels and presents Christ Jesus as the high priest who made the perfect sacrifice freely given to all who will accept it on their behalf. These essential doctrines are also found in other New Testament books. Hebrews addresses and refutes the major arguments against Christ being the Messiah. The writer of Hebrews exalts Jesus as superior to anything that preceded Him, including the law, prophets, sacrifices, and any form of priesthood. All are deficient in comparison to Christ Jesus, who is presented as the perfect sacrifice, the perfect high priest, the only Savior, and the Son of God.

The book appears to have been intended for Christian Jews who had been exposed to both social and physical persecution from both Jews and Gentiles, although none had yet died for the faith (Heb. 12:4). It also appears that the recipients of the letter had hesitated to separate themselves completely from Judaism, perhaps because their ties to Judaism allowed them some protection under Roman law and they feared the consequences a total commitment to Christ might bring. This scenario could easily apply to Jewish Christians in Rome as they approached the time of persecution under emperor Nero, but this is speculation (Heb. 13:24). Whatever may have caused their reluctance, the recipients of the letter appear to have been wavering in their commitment to Christ. The author of the letter admonished them to renew their confidence in Jesus Christ, encouraged them to persevere, and exhorted them to mature in their faith. The book has been dated between 64 and 70 AD, on the basis of persecutions already endured and those predicted.

Hebrews presents the clearest discussion of the Christian understanding of the Old Testament found in the New Testament. It provides a fairly extensive look at the Jewish sacrificial system and priesthood—the religious sacrifices referenced relate to the Old Testament tabernacle, rather than the temple (Heb. 8 –10). The author quotes the Old Testament extensively, especially the book of Psalms, and uses the major Greek translation of the Hebrew Old Testament (Septuagint). The law of Moses and the prophecies of the Old Testament are portrayed as pointing undeniably to Christ and as being fulfilled by Him.

Hebrews not only examines critical theological issues, but it provides very direct warnings and challenges to all Christians: don't fall short of all God has for you, be encouraged that God's Word is powerful and Christ is interceding for you, and continue to run with endurance the race that has been set before you—all the way to perfection.

About the Author. Scholars through the centuries have suggested a number of possible authors for Hebrews including Paul, Luke, Clement of Rome, Phillip, Priscilla, Barnabas, and Apollos. We do not know with certainty, however, who the author may have been.

What we can conclude from the book of Hebrews itself is that the author was very likely trained in Greek oratory. The opening sentences of Hebrews are the most sonorous piece of Greek in the entire New Testament. It is a passage any classical Greek orator would have been proud to claim. We can also conclude that the author had studied the Old Testament in depth, as well as Jewish intertestamental literature (sometimes called the Apocrypha), since the book contains numerous references to images and principles in those writings.

An Overview of Our Study
of the Epistle to the Hebrews

This study guide presents seven lessons drawn from the epistle to the Hebrews. It elaborates upon, and is based upon the commentary included in the *Blackaby Study Bible*:

Lesson #1: Jesus, the Heir of All Things

Lesson #2: Jesus, Our Suffering Savior

Lesson #3: Jesus, Our High Priest Forever

Lesson #4: Jesus, Surety of a Better Covenant

Lesson #5: Faith That Obtains a Good Testimony

Lesson #6: Running the Faith Race

Lesson #7: Becoming Complete

Personal or Group Use. These lessons are offered for personal study and reflection or for small-group Bible study. The study questions may be answered by an individual reader or used as a foundation for group discussion. A segment titled "Notes to Leaders of Small Groups" is included at the back of this book to help those leading a group study of material.

Before you embark on this study, we encourage you to read in full the statement in the *Blackaby Study Bible* titled "How to Study the Bible." Our contention is that the Bible is unique among all literature. It is God's definitive word for humanity. The Bible is

- *inspired*—"God-breathed"

- *authoritative*—absolutely the final word on any spiritual matter

- *the plumb line of truth*—the standard against which all human activity and reasoning must be evaluated

The Bible is fascinating in that it has remarkable diversity but also remarkable unity. Its books were penned by a diverse assortment of authors representing a variety of languages and cultures, and it contains a number of literary forms. But the Bible's message from cover to cover is clear, consistent, and unified.

More than mere words on a page, the Bible is an encounter with God Himself. No book is more critical to your life. The very essence of the Bible is the Lord Himself.

The Holy Spirit speaks through the Bible. He also communicates during your time of prayer, in your life circumstances, and through the church. Read your Bible in an attitude of prayer, and allow the Holy Spirit to make you aware of God's activity in and through your personal life. Write down what you learn, meditate on it, and adjust your thoughts, attitudes, and behavior accordingly. Look for ways every day to apply the truth of God's Word to your circumstances and relationships. God is not random; He is orderly and intentional in the way He speaks to you.

Be encouraged—the Bible is *not* too difficult for the average person to understand if that person asks the Holy Spirit for help. (Furthermore, not even the most brilliant person can fully understand the Bible apart from the Holy Spirit's help!) God desires for you to know Him and to know His Word. Every person who reads the Bible can learn from it. The person who will receive *maximum* benefit from reading and studying the Bible, however, is the person who:

- *is born again* (John 3:3,5). Those who are born again and have received the gift of His Spirit have a distinct advantage in understanding the deeper truths of God's Word.
- *has a heart that desires to learn God's truth.* Your attitude influences greatly the outcome of Bible study. Resist the temptation to focus on what others have said about the Bible. Allow the Holy Spirit to guide you as you study God's Word for yourself.
- *has a heart that seeks to obey God.* The Holy Spirit teaches the most to those who desire to apply what they learn.

Begin your Bible study with prayer, asking the Holy Spirit to guide your thoughts and to impress upon you what is on God's heart. Then, make plans to adjust your life immediately to obey the Lord fully.

As you read and study the Bible, your purpose is not to *create* meaning, but to *discover* the meaning of the text with the Holy Spirit's guidance. Ask yourself, "What did the author have in mind? How was this applied by those who first heard these words?"

At times you may find it helpful to consult other passages of the Bible (made available in the center columns in the *Blackaby Study Bible*), or the commentary that is in the margins of the *Blackaby Study Bible*.

Keep in mind always that Bible study is not primarily an exercise for acquiring information but an opportunity for transformation. Bible study is your opportunity to encounter God and to be changed in His presence. When God speaks to your heart, nothing remains the same. Jesus said, "He who has ears to hear, let him hear" (Matt. 13:9). Choose to have ears that desire to hear!

The B-A-S-I-Cs of Each Study in This Guide. Each lesson in this study guide has five segments, using the word BASIC as an acronym. The word BASIC does not allude to elementary or simple, but rather, to foundational. These studies extend the concepts that are part of the *Blackaby Study Bible* commentary and are focused on key aspects of what it means to be a Christ-follower in today's world. The BASIC acronym stands for:

B = Bible Focus. This segment presents the central passage for the lesson and a general explanation that covers the central theme or concern.

A = Application for Today. This segment has a story or illustration related to modern-day times, with questions that link the Bible text to today's issues, problems, and concerns.

S = Supplementary Scriptures to Consider. In this segment other Bible verses related to the general theme of the lesson are explored.

I = Introspection and Implications. In this segment questions are asked that lead to deeper reflection about one's personal faith journey and life experiences.

C = Communicating the Good News. In this segment challenging questions point to ways the lesson's truth might be lived out and shared with others, whether to win the lost or build up the church.

LESSON #1

JESUS, THE HEIR
OF ALL THINGS

*Heir: the right, by law, to receive property, position,
or title from another after that person dies*

B
Bible Focus

> *God, who at various times and in various ways spoke in*
> *time past to the fathers by the prophets, has in these last days*
> *spoken to us by His Son, whom He has appointed heir of all*
> *things, through whom also He made the worlds; who being the*
> *brightness of His glory and the express image of His person,*
> *and upholding all things by the word of His power, when He*
> *had by Himself purged our sins, sat down at the right hand of*
> *the Majesty on high, having become so much better than the*
> *angels, as He has by inheritance obtained a more excellent*
> *name than they. . . .*
> *For in that He put all in subjection under him, He left*
> *nothing that is not put under him (Heb. 1:1–4,2:8).*

The writer of Hebrews opened his message with two tremendous truths. First, God speaks both to create and to uphold what He has created. This truth is embodied fully in Christ Jesus, the incarnate Word of God.

The Jewish people had worshiped God as Creator for thousands of years prior to the birth of Jesus. They had a firm understanding that God had spoken the universe into existence and that His ongoing word allowed the universe to exist and remain in balance.

They also readily believed that God had spoken His divine will to chosen prophets, who in turn spoke God's word to the Israelites. The Jews believed strongly that the prophets were highly privileged in knowing the secret counsels of God: "Surely the Lord God does nothing, unless He reveals His secrets to His servants the prophets" (Amos 3). It was through the prophetic word that God established or created His will among His people, and upheld or maintained His commandments and principles as absolute truth.

It was a new concept for the Jews, however, to regard Jesus as the incarnate Word of God—the second member of the Trinity who was the active agent of God's creation. It was the Word of God that proclaimed, "Let there be. . . . " It was the Word of God who, at His death by crucifixion, said, "It is finished." In the mind and hearts of the apostles and all who followed Him as disciples, Jesus was established as the "first and last," the Alpha and Omega, the beginning and ending of all God desired to create and maintain as truth. Jesus is presented throughout the New Testament as the firstborn of God's new spiritual creation.

As the incarnate Word of God, Jesus is far superior to a prophet. The full impact of His message was not bound to words or to dramatic action, as were the messages of the ancient prophets. His message was embodied by a life that was a full and complete revelation of God's glory and the fullness of God's character.

It is by believing in Jesus as God's Son that a person is re-created or born again as a new spiritual creature. It is by following Jesus and serving Him as Lord that a person maintains a close relationship with God and matures spiritually.

God's Word is powerful beyond our imagining or understanding. And because the Holy Spirit of God indwells the Christian, our words spoken in the name of Jesus take on a spiritual dimension to create and uphold what is right, pure, good, and true.

The second main truth in these opening sentences of Hebrews conveys the concept that He who creates, owns. Christ Jesus, the Word present at the creation of all things in the natural world, owns the natural world. During His earthly ministry, Jesus displayed on numerous occasions His power over nature, from the multiplication of loaves and fishes, to walking on water, to commanding storms to cease, to healing disease. He displayed His spiritual ownership of all things through His command over demons, the devil, and death and, ultimately, in His own atoning death on the cross and resurrection from the dead. Those of us who believe in Christ's death on our behalf and who have received Jesus as Savior are owned by Christ—we belong to Him forever. All things are in subjection to Him. He is the owner and heir of all that He has created, possesses, and maintains!

How does this impact us today?

There are countless people, including many in the church, who question whether God speaks to mankind. The writer of Hebrews would respond, "God's greatest message continues to be the one embodied in Christ Jesus— who bore fully the glory of God's image." The real question is not whether God speaks but whether we are listening to what God is saying to us in Christ.

What is God speaking to *you* today about who Christ is, who you are in Christ, and what God desires to say to the world through *your* life in Christ? Are you allowing Christ to create in you His own character likeness?

There are also many people who are troubled by the idea that, as Christians, they no longer have any right of ownership over themselves. We live in a society that calls to each of us, "Be your own person." God's Word, in sharp contrast, calls upon us to "be Christ's person" and to reflect Him to the world.

Do you have any qualms about being owned by Christ Jesus?

A
Application for Today

"What did you get?" the children asked their father eagerly when he returned from a meeting at the family attorney's office where the meeting had been one in which the will of an unmarried aunt was read.

The father gathered the family around him and said, "Let me share with you what her will says. As you know, I have two sisters and two first cousins. All five of us were there, and she left something to each of us."

"Aunt Bea noted that Sally had always extended great kindness to her, and she stated in her will that she wanted five thousand dollars to be given in Sally's name to a local charity that is known for acts of kindness. She said, 'Acts of kindness should go on.'

"Aunt Bea noted that Brenda has always been filled with interesting conversation, and in later years had come to read to Aunt Bea when her eyesight failed. She stated in the will that that she wanted five thousand dollars to be given in Brenda's name to a particular school. She said, 'Learning is important and should continue.'

"Aunt Bea noted that she hadn't seen Fred and Gary for many years, and she realized they had been busy working and providing for their families. She stated in her will that she wanted them each to be given what amounted to two days paid vacation from their jobs so they might spend some time with their children who now live out of state."

"But what about *you*, Dad," the children asked eagerly. "Aunt Bea wrote that she appreciated the times we visited her as a family and prayed with her and shared with her what God was doing in our lives. She admired greatly our involvement in the church and our going as a family on short-term missions trips through the church. She left the rest of her estate to our church as a trust set up in her name and mine. The trust is to provide scholarships for youth mission trips."

The children seemed disappointed. "So you didn't get anything," one of the boys finally said.

"To the contrary!" Dad replied. "I don't see it that way at all! Aunt Bea gave me her blessing and an opportunity to be a blessing. There's no greater inheritance I could have received from her!"

How would you have felt if you had been one of Aunt Bea's heirs?

Hebrews states that Jesus is the heir of all that belongs to God the Father. What is it that Jesus inherited?

As a Christian, you are part of Jesus' inheritance! What did Jesus get when He inherited *you*?

S
Supplementary Scriptures to Consider

The apostle Paul taught that because we belong to Christ and we are indwelled by His Holy Spirit, we are joint heirs with Christ:

> The Spirit Himself bears witness with our spirit that we are children of God, and if children, then heirs—heirs of God and joint heirs with Christ, if indeed we suffer with Him, that we may also be glorified together (Romans 8:16-17).

• What do you believe you have inherited as a "child of God" and "joint heir with Christ"?

mercy
grace
kindness
lack of needs - for they are provided
forgiveness

• Is there anything that you believe Christ has inherited that you have *not* inherited jointly with Him? If so, what is it? If not, why not?

ability to do signs and wonders

The apostle Paul wrote to the Ephesians about Christ's authority over all things:

> Therefore I also, after I heard of your faith in the Lord Jesus and your love for all the saints, do not cease to give thanks for you, making mention of you in my prayers: that the God our Lord Jesus Christ, the Father of glory, may give to you the spirit of wisdom and revelation in the knowledge of

Him, the eyes of your understanding being enlightened; that
you may know what is the hope of His calling, what are the
riches of the glory of His inheritance in the saints, and what is
the exceeding greatness of His power toward us who believe,
according to the working of His mighty power which He
worked in Christ when He raised Him from the dead and
seated Him at His right hand in the heavenly places, far above
all principality and power and might and dominion, and every
name that is named, not only in this age but also in what
which is to come.

And He put all things under His feet and gave Him to be
head over all things to the church, which is His body, the
fullness of Him who fills all in all" (Eph. 1:15–23).

• What does the phrase "riches of the glory of His inheritance in the saints"
mean to you? Do you fully regard yourself as a saint in line to receive the
riches of glory of His inheritance?

I am undeserving and a sinner

• Are there things in your personal life that you do not believe are fully
subject to Christ? If so, what do you believe God desires for you to do?
What do you believe He has promised to do on your behalf?

give them to Him
be with me always

The apostle Paul also wrote to the Galatians about being an heir of God through Christ:

> If you are Christ's, then you are Abraham's seed, and heirs according to the promise. . . . When the fullness of the time had come, God sent forth His Son, born of a woman, born under the law, to redeem those who were under the law, that we might receive the adoption as sons. And because you are sons, God has sent forth the Spirit of His Son into your hearts, crying out, "Abba, Father!" Therefore you are no longer a slave but a son, and if a son, then an heir of God through Christ (Gal. 3:29, 4:4–7).

• Is there a difference in being owned by God as a slave and being owned by God as a son?

God has No slaves only children

A Roman centurion sought out Jesus to ask that Jesus heal his servant who was paralyzed and "dreadfully tormented." Jesus agreed to accompany the centurion back to his dwelling place.

> The centurion answered and said, "Lord, I am not worthy that You should come under my roof. But only speak a word, and my servant will be healed. For I also am a man under authority, having soldiers under me. And I say to this one, 'Go,' and he goes; and to another, 'Come,' and he comes; and to my servant, 'Do this,' and he does it."
> When Jesus heard it, He marveled and said to those who followed, "Assuredly, I say to you. I have not found such great faith, not even in Israel!" . . . Then Jesus said to the centurion, "Go your way; and as you have believed, so let it be done for ✗ you." And his servant was healed that same hour" (Matt. 8:8–10, 13).

- What did Jesus create by His words in this passage of scripture? What did He create by His words at other times in His earthly ministry?

- Does Jesus still speak today from His position at the right hand of the Father? Is His message the same from heaven as it was on this earth?

- In what ways do you struggle with believing that God may be speaking words from heaven today for *your* healing or blessing, or for the healing or blessing of someone you love?

• How do we hear Jesus speaking to us, "As you have believed, so let it be done for you"?

The Bible - God's Word

I
Introspection and Implications

1. In what ways is it important to you as you pray to believe that Jesus is the rightfully appointed "heir of all things" and that all things are in subjection to Him? Can a person pray effectively and expectantly without believing that Jesus has authority over all aspects of the material and spiritual realms?

2. In what ways is it important to your personal faith in Christ to believe that Jesus is the "brightness of [God the Father's] glory and the express image of His person"?

3. The Hebrew word for glory, *kabod*, means "heavy in weight." To give someone glory was to give him great honor, to consider that the substance of His being had supreme value. The Greek word is *doxa*, which means to give an opinion or an estimate, an honor that comes from a high opinion of others. In what way do you seek to give God glory?

C
Communicating the Good News

A significant number of people in our world today believe that Jesus was a prophet but not the Son of God. They believe He was an excellent man and good moral teacher, but not divine, and not the Savior. How do you respond to those who hold such opinions?

How important is the supremacy of Christ to our presentation of the gospel message? In what ways is the supremacy of Christ central to all evangelism? Consider these questions:

• If Christ Jesus is not *the* Way, why should he even be considered to be *a* way (John 14:6)?

• In what ways does the Bible present the truth that Jesus is superior to all other men who ever lived?

• Why is Jesus more than just another martyr for a good cause?

Joyce Meyer
Heb 9:12-17
Tell the Devel you are none of his buseness

LESSON #2

JESUS, OUR SUFFERING SAVIOR

Captain: leader with formal command

Propitiation: the force of reconciliation or appeasement

B
Bible Focus

> *We see Jesus, who was made a little lower than the angels,*
> *for the suffering of death crowned with glory and honor, that*
> *He, by the grace of God, might taste death for everyone.*
> *For it was fitting for Him, for whom are all things and by*
> *whom are all things, in bringing many sons to glory, to make*
> *the captain of their salvation perfect through sufferings. . . .*
> *Inasmuch then as the children have partaken of flesh and*
> *blood, He Himself likewise shared in the same, that through*
> *death He might destroy him who had the power of death, that*
> *is, the devil, and release those who through fear of death were*
> *all their lifetime subject to bondage. For indeed He does not*
> *give aid to angels, but He does give aid to the seed of Abra-*
> *ham. Therefore, in all things He had to be made like His*
> *brethren, that He might be a merciful and faithful High Priest*
> *in things pertaining to God, to make propitiation for the sins*
> *of the people. For in that He Himself has suffered, being*
> *tempted, He is able to aid those who are tempted*
> *(Heb. 2:9–10, 14–18).*

The death of Jesus on the cross was a suffering death. That fact was problematic for both the Jews and the Greeks. Glory and suffering were regarded as the opposite ends of a spectrum. If Jesus reflected the brightness of God's glory, how could He suffer? How could God's grace include a cruel and dishonorable form of death? Indeed, how could the suffering of death be crowned with glory and honor? How could the captain of our salvation be made perfect through suffering?

In addressing such questions, the writer of Hebrews summed up his rationale with one word: propitiation.

The pagan Greeks and Romans had a concept of propitiation as a bribe for a deity. That is *not* the biblical use of the word! This Bible word refers to a sacrifice that satisfies God's standard for justice and his requirement for turning away His wrath, which our sin rightfully incurs. The Jews knew that the price of sin was death and separation from God. This teaching is throughout the Old Testament and was stated by the apostle Paul clearly in his letter to the Romans: "For the wages of sin is death, but the gift of God is eternal life" (Rom. 6:23).

For the sin of mankind to be forgiven and relationship to be fully restored between God and mankind, God required a *perfect* sacrifice—a sinless, guileless sacrifice—and this could only be satisfied fully by the sacrifice of Himself, His Son Jesus. "For God so loved the world that He gave His only begotten Son, that whoever believes in Him should not perish but have everlasting life" (John 3:16). Hebrews states that it is for this very purpose of being propitiation that Jesus was made a little lower than the angels—a human being. God identified with mankind *fully*—but without sin–in order to die on man's behalf, so that mankind might identify *fully* with Him and live forever.

Hebrews states that, in addition to being the propitiation for our sin, Jesus accomplished three things through his suffering death:

First, Jesus destroyed the power of death held by the devil. The devil had tempted Adam and Eve with fruit from the tree of the knowledge of good and evil, lying to them when he said they would not die. In aspiring to be as wise as God, they ate and faced the certain consequences God had foretold: "you *shall* surely die" (See Gen. 2:17 and 3:1–19). From the Garden of Eden until this present time, the devil has sought to convince men and women to do things their way, according to their human standards of what is right and wrong. People who succumb to the devil's temptation to do things their way, rather than trust God and obey His way, are destroyed. Jesus made it very clear that only God's way should be considered when He declared, "I am the way [of salvation, forgiveness, and reconciliation with the Father], the truth [of everything you ever need to know], and the life [everlasting]" (John 14:6).

Certainly every human being dies; nobody escapes natural death. But the real "power of death" the devil holds is his power to tempt mankind to do whatever it takes to avoid *suffering* and to seek an alternative way to live and to gain heaven. Jesus destroyed that power in the Garden of Gethsemane. When the devil came to Him one final time with a temptation to sidestep the suffering of crucifixion and momentary separation from the Father, Jesus prayed, "If it is possible, let this cup pass from Me." When He realized that the cup of suffering was the cup required, He said, "Nevertheless, not as I will but as You will." We may suffer in this life, but if that is the case, we can be assured that God has a great purpose for our suffering, a great reward awaiting us, and that our suffering will not have been in vain. We must never abandon Christ in hopes of finding an alternative easy way out.

Second, Jesus destroyed the fear of death that keeps people in bondage. The fear of death comes when people believe that death is "final" and there is no eternity, or that they have sinned and cannot receive eternal life. Jesus' resurrection is total affirmation that human natural death for the Christian is only a transitory moment to a greater and more glorious life in eternity.

Third, having been tempted through suffering, Jesus became fully qualified to give aid to all who suffer and are tempted. Jesus knows what you are feeling or going through. He's been there!

What does the suffering of Jesus mean to you personally?

What might be the purpose of suffering in the life of a Christian?

— *God has a purpose* —

A
Application for Today

Trouble seemed to pile onto trouble for Rick: the death of a coworker, an accident that resulted in a permanent injury, loss of full-time employment, financial strain. Rick told his pastor, "You name it, I got it."

The troubles turned into depression, and after several months Rick's wife, several other family members, their pastor, and a close friend all agreed that Rick *must* seek help. Rick resisted this suggestion for several more weeks, but finally his sadness became so overwhelming that he made an appointment to see his family physician. The physician ran a number of medical tests to determine if the cause of Rick's depression was physiological. When the tests came back normal, the physician recommended Rick visit with a psychological counselor. Although Rick was reluctant to do this, he finally made an appointment.

Rick's wife, Ann, eagerly awaited his return from the appointment. "How did it go?" she asked as soon as he walked in the door.

"He can't help me," Rick said with sadness in his voice, not criticism or rejection.

"Why do you say that?" Ann replied. "You've only been to see him one time and only for an hour."

"I just know," Rick said.

"But *how* do you know," his wife insisted.

"Cuz I asked him some questions about *his* life," Rick said, "and he ain't been through nuthin'."

Who is the better counselor, the person who has suffered or the person who has not?

Who is the better comforter, the person who has suffered or the person who has not?

Who is the greater source of inspiration and encouragement in a time of trouble, the person who has suffered or the person who has not?

S
Supplementary Scriptures to Consider

Later in the book of Hebrews, we find these statements about Christ's suffering:

> Though He was a Son, yet He learned obedience by the things which He suffered. And having been perfected, He became the author of eternal salvation to all who obey Him (Heb. 5:8–9).

• What do these verses tell us about the lesson associated with suffering?

• What have you learned from a time of suffering in *your* life? (Note: Focus on one particular incident or condition.) Were the lessons you learned related to obedience to God? In what ways?

• In what ways does suffering perfect a person? (Note: To perfect is to "make whole" or to "complete.")

Hebrews draws a correlation between a faithful believer's suffering and a good testimony:

> Others were tortured, not accepting deliverance, that they might obtain a better resurrection. Still others had trial of mockings and scourgings, yes, and of chains and imprisonment. They were stoned, they were sawn in two, were tempted, were slain with the sword. They wandered about in sheepskins and goatskins, being destitute, afflicted, tormented—of whom the world was not worthy. They wandered in deserts and mountains, in dens and caves of the earth. And all these, having obtained a good testimony through faith. . . . (Heb. 11:35–39).

• How does a person's faith help that person withstand the pain of suffering?

• Note that Hebrews acknowledges that mocking and tempting are forms of suffering. Have you ever suffered as a result of being mocked or publicly tempted, humiliated, or tormented? How did you respond? What happened as a result?

• Hebrews notes that some who were tortured were offered a way out of their torture—most likely a reference to being offered a release from torture for denying Jesus as the Christ—but they turned down the offer in order to obtain a greater reward. Have we lost sight of a martyr's reward in our world today? Have you considered what *you* would do if you were being tortured and you were offered release for denying Christ as your Savior? What about if your beloved child was being tortured and you were offered release for your child in exchange for denying Jesus?

Jesus taught:

> "Blessed are you when they revile and persecute you, and say all kinds of evil against you falsely for My sake. Rejoice and be exceedingly glad, for great is your reward in heaven, for so they persecuted the prophets who were before you" (Matt. 5:11–12).

• Why is it important that your persecutions and sufferings be for the cause of Christ, rather than your own mistakes or lack of good judgment? How do we know that we are being reviled or persecuted for our *faith*?

Peter wrote this to a group of believers who were living in a time of intense persecution:

> Beloved, do not think it strange concerning the fiery trial
> which is to try you, as though some strange thing happened to
> you; but rejoice to the extent that you partake of Christ's
> sufferings, that when His glory is revealed, you may also be
> glad with exceeding joy. If you are reproached for the name of
> Christ, blessed are you, for the Spirit of glory and of God rests
> upon you. . . . But let none of you suffer as a murderer, a
> thief, an evildoer, or as a busybody in other people's matters.
> Yet if anyone suffers as a Christian, let him not be ashamed,
> but let him glorify God in this matter (1 Peter 4:12–16).

• Why do Christians today in many sectors of the church seem to *expect* to avoid all suffering or persecution because they are Christians? Is it right or wrong to have such an expectation? Why so?

• Do you know of a person who has been criticized because he has suffered for Christ? What about a person who has been reproached for the sins of a spouse or child, or perhaps has been persecuted because of a sinning spouse filing for divorce?

• How can a person practically and wholeheartedly glorify God in a time of persecution?

I
Introspection and Implications

1. Consider what your response would be to a person who asked you, "Why did Jesus have to die?"

2. Has your suffering in life made you more empathetic and compassionate toward other people who may be facing what you have been through? How so?

3. If you don't believe you've ever faced a time of genuine suffering or pain, do you believe that you might face such a time in your future? If so, how are you preparing your own heart and seeking to strengthen your faith for such a time?

4. Do you expect to face more suffering or less suffering in your future? On the basis of what?

5. Do you fear death? If so, do you know why you have this fear? If not, why not?

6. Do you fear suffering? How do you face that fear?

C
Communicating the Good News

What is it that we can promise to an unbeliever *with certainty*?

Why is it wrong to offer an unbeliever a life in Christ that results in all roses, no thorns?

What is the message of hope we have to offer an unbeliever who may be experiencing a serious illness, great pain, or some other form of suffering?

LESSON #3

JESUS, OUR
HIGH PRIEST FOREVER

High Priest: the head of all the priests in Judaism in the days of the tabernacle and temple; the one responsible for standing before God daily and for offering the annual sacrifice of atonement

B
Bible Focus

> Seeing then that we have a great High Priest who has passed through the heavens, Jesus the Son of God, let us hold fast our confession. For we do not have a High Priest who cannot sympathize with our weaknesses, but was in all points tempted as we are, yet without sin. Let us therefore come boldly to the throne of grace, that we may obtain mercy and find grace to help in time of need.
>
> For every high priest taken from among men is appointed for men in things pertaining to God, that he may offer both gifts and sacrifices for sins. He can have compassion on those who are ignorant and going astray, since he himself is also subject to weakness. Because of this he is required as for the people, so also for himself, to offer sacrifices for sins. And no man takes this honor to himself, but he who is called by God, just as Aaron was.
>
> So also Christ did not glorify Himself to become High Priest, but it was He who said to Him:
>
> "You are My Son,
>
> Today I have begotten You."
>
> As He also says in another place:
>
> "You are a priest forever
>
> According to the order of Melchizedek". . . .
>
> For every high priest is appointed to offer both gifts and sacrifices. Therefore it is necessary that this One also have something to offer. For if He were on earth, He would not be a priest, since there are priests who offer the gifts according to the law; who serve the copy and shadow of the heavenly things, as Moses was divinely instructed when he was about to make the tabernacle. . . But now He has obtained a more excellent ministry, inasmuch as He is also Mediator of a better covenant, which was established on better promises
> (Heb. 4:14, 5:6, 8:3–6)

Jesus was from the tribe of Judah, a tribe that had nothing to do with the ancient Jewish priesthood. On what basis, then, did Jesus assume all authority as a high priest? The writer to the Hebrews said this: "In the likeness of

Melchizedek, there arises another priest who has come, not according to the law of a fleshly commandment, but according to the power of an endless life" (Heb. 7:15–16).

Who is Melchizedek? He is first mentioned in the Bible in Genesis 14 in association with Abraham, who was still called Abram at that point. A tremendous battle—four kings against five—took place in the Valley of Siddim, near the cities of Sodom and Gomorrah. Abram's nephew Lot and all of Lot's possessions were taken captive. A person who escaped the onslaught immediately went to Abram, and when Abram heard his nephew had been taken, he armed 318 of his trained servants and pursued of the conquering armies. Through clever military tactics, this relatively small band of men freed Lot and his goods, as well as the women and others who had been taken captive.

When they returned to the King's Valley, they were met by both the king of Sodom and Melchizedek, who is described as the king of Salem. Salem is the ancient name for Jerusalem, which is likely a reference to nearby Jerusalem. His name means "my king is righteousness" and his title refers to "king of peace." Like Abram, Melchizedek worshiped the true and living God. He is described in Genesis as "the priest of God Most High."

As part of the homecoming ceremony, Melchizedek brought out bread and wine and blessed Abraham, saying,

"Blessed be Abram of God Most High,

Possessor of heaven and earth;

And blessed be God Most High,

Who has delivered your enemies into your hand" (Gen. 14:18–20).

Abraham, in return, gave Melchizedek a tenth, or tithe, of all he had.

Melchizedek's description as a priest mediating between mankind and God Most High, his blessing of Abram, his acceptance of a tithe of the captured goods, and his use of bread and wine—the elements of Communion—have led many scholars to consider Melchizedek as an appearance of the preincarnate Christ.

In what ways was Melchizedek different from the priests associated with Aaron and the law of Moses? Melchizedek was appointed by God, not by human bloodline. Melchizedek, as God's representative, initiated the ceremony of blessing. He brought out the sacrificial elements and gave them to Abram. In the Jewish priestly system, the elements of sacrifice were brought by the people and then, through the priest, offered to God on a regular human timetable, some daily, some weekly, some annually.

Jesus was sent by God, not appointed or elected by men. He was God's only begotten Son, sent on a divine mission of forgiveness and mercy to a sin-sick and dying world (John 3:16).

Jesus initiated blessing to us. He loved us while we were still sinners and died for us. As 1 John 4:19 says, "We love Him because He first loved us." Jesus initiated the Last Supper and said, "As often as you do this, remember Me."

The writer to the Hebrews indicated that Melchizedek is a priest forever— the eternal priest of God—and that Jesus fulfills this role as our mediator and Savior. The rolling back of sin through priest-offered sacrifices was temporary. The genuine forgiveness of sin through Christ is eternal.

Earlier in the book of Hebrews, the writer pointed to the supremacy of Christ over all prophets in Israel's past. He pointed in chapter 2 to Christ's supremacy over the angels of heaven. He gave reason for Christ to be worthy of all glory and honor, even as a suffering and dying Savior. And in this passage, the writer of Hebrews declared the supremacy of Christ over all priests in Israel's past. A logical, point-by-point case is being made: Jesus *is* Lord! He alone is our Savior worthy to be worshiped and adored.

What does it mean to you personally that Christ took the initiative in extending love and forgiveness to you, that He came in search of you, even before you felt a need for Him as your Savior?

A
Application for Today

"Who is your priest?" Georgia asked Alice, a woman she had met the previous weekend at a business seminar. The two seemed to have a lot in common, and they had agreed to have dinner together to get better acquainted.

"Oh, I don't have a priest," Alice said. "I'm not Catholic . . . or Anglican. I have a pastor, not a priest."

Georgia smiled, "I'm not Catholic or Anglican either. But I have a priest."

"Why?" Alice asked.

"Because a priest is someone who makes a sacrifice to God on behalf of the people and who intercedes in praying to God for the people God has put under him," Georgia explained.

"I don't need a priest to do that for me," Alice said boldly. "Jesus Christ did that for me. He died as the sacrifice for my sin, and the Bible says He is praying for me always at the right hand of God the Father."

"Right!" said Georgia. "My point exactly. Jesus is your priest. I'm so glad to know that. He's my priest, too!"

"Are you telling me that we're both Christians?" Alice asked.

"Absolutely!" said Georgia.

"That's great!" Alice said. "I suspected you were a Christian. But why didn't you just say so? Why bring up all that stuff about a priest?"

"I was just having a little fun," Georgia said, "trying to discover more about your faith. I have a confession to make: I went to a Bible study on the book of Hebrews last night, and the lesson was about Jesus being our high priest."

"Confession?" Alice quipped. "Don't tell me! Go tell a priest!"

What does it mean to you that Christ Jesus is your high priest?

S
Supplementary Scriptures to Consider

The writer of the book of Hebrews reminded his readers of the priest-offered sacrifices initiated by Moses:

> The priests always went into the first part of the tabernacle, performing the services. But into the second part the high priest went alone once a year, not without blood, which he offered for himself and for the people's sins committed in ignorance; the Holy Spirit indicating this, that the way into the Holiest of All was not yet made manifest while the first tabernacle was still standing. It was symbolic for the present time in which both the gifts and sacrifices are offered which cannot make him who performed the service perfect in regard to the conscience—concerned only with foods and drinks, various washings, and fleshly ordinances imposed until the time of reformation . . .
>
> If the blood of bulls and goats and the ashes of a heifer, sprinkling the unclean, sanctifies for the purifying of the flesh, how much more shall the blood of Christ, who through the eternal Spirit offered Himself without spot to God, cleanse your conscience from dead works to serve the living God (Heb. 9:6–10, 13–14)?

• The Jewish people from the beginning had a strong understanding that blood is a symbol of *life*. They were acutely aware that God had made a blood sacrifice and clothed Adam and Eve in the skins of the slain animals as a reminder that there is no life without blood. Why was it necessary for Jesus to shed His blood as part of His atoning sacrifice for our sin? How does the shedding of His blood relate to our being given *eternal* life when we accept Jesus as our Savior?

• In this lesson's opening passages from Hebrews, a reference is made to things associated with the law serving as a "copy and shadow of the heavenly things" in Moses' instructions for the tabernacle. How do you believe this relates to the blood sacrifices and offerings of the tabernacle?

Those who came to Christ out of Judaism nearly always were forced to leave their synagogues. They frequently were disowned by their families. Keep that in mind as you read this passage from Hebrews:

> We have an altar from which those who serve the tabernacle have no right to eat. For the bodies of those animals, whose blood is brought into the sanctuary by the high priest for sin, are burned outside the camp. Therefore Jesus also, that He might sanctify the people with His own blood, suffered outside the gate. Therefore let us go forth to Him, outside the camp, bearing His reproach. For here we have no continuing city, but we seek the one to come. Therefore by Him let us continually offer the sacrifice of praise to God, that is, the fruit of our lips, giving thanks to His name (Heb. 13:10–15).

• Jesus was crucified outside the city gates of Jerusalem. Why is it necessary, as Hebrews says, for some people to go outside their current
religious home in order to worship Christ fully and freely?

• In what ways is praise a sacrifice to God?

• What does it mean to bear reproach for the cause of Christ? If we
have never experienced this, how do we prepare ourselves for the
potential of experiencing it?

The book of Psalms also has a reference to the Messiah being a priest
forever according to the order of Melchizedek:

> The LORD said to my Lord,
> "Sit at My right hand,
> Till I make Your enemies Your footstool."
> The LORD shall send the rod of Your strength out of Zion.
> Rule in the midst of Your enemies!
> Your people shall be volunteers
> In the day of Your power;

> In the beauties of holiness, from the womb of the morning,
> You have the dew of Your youth.
> The LORD has sword
> And will not relent,
> "You are a priest forever
> According to the order of Melchizedek" (Ps. 110:1–4).

- Why was it important for first-century Jewish Christians to believe that Jesus was their high priest?

- Why was it important for Jesus *not* to come from a line of human priests? Why is that important to those of us who come to Christ as Gentiles today?

- What are the promises made to the priest identified in Psalm 110? What cause does this give you for praising Jesus today?

I

Introspection and Implications

1. Respond to this statement from Hebrews: "For we do not have a High Priest who cannot sympathize with our weaknesses, but was in all points tempted as we are, yet without sin" (Heb. 4:15). What difference does it make to you to know that Jesus was tempted in the same ways you are as a human being, but didn't sin? What does it mean to you that Jesus is able to sympathize with your weaknesses?

2. Respond to this statement from Hebrews: "Let us therefore come boldly to the throne of grace, that we may obtain mercy and find grace to help in time of need" (Heb. 4:16). Have you ever gone to God in a time of weakness or temptation to ask boldly and immediately for God's help? What happened? What does it mean to you to "obtain mercy and find grace to help" in a time of need?

3. The writer to Hebrews noted that it is an honor to be a priest and that "no man takes this honor to himself, but he who is called by God" (Heb. 5:4). How do you discern whether a person is taking the honor of priestly ministry to himself or is acting on a definite call of God? How do you determine in your own life if an area of ministry is something you desire to do or something God is calling you to do?

C
Communicating the Good News

In what ways do you struggle with believing that God is pursuing your unsaved loved ones in a proactive, diligent, and loving manner, especially when you don't see any evidence of His pursuit?

What is the balance in being patient as God woos a lost soul to Himself and abdicating all responsibility for soul-winning because you believe God will find a way to reach each person?

Lesson #4

JESUS, SURETY OF A BETTER COVENANT

Surety: somebody who assumes responsibility for another's obligations in case of default, giving a guarantee

Covenant: a solemn, formal, legally binding agreement

B
Bible Focus

> *Jesus has become a surety of a better covenant. . . .*
>
> *For if that first covenant had been faultless, then no place would have been sought for a second. Because finding fault with them, He says, "Behold, the days are coming, says the LORD, when I will make a new covenant with the house of Israel and with the house of Judah—not according to the covenant that I made with their fathers in the day when I took them by the hand to lead them out of the land of Egypt; because they did not continue in My covenant, and I disregarded them, says the LORD. For this is the covenant that I will make with the house of Israel after those days, says the LORD: I will put My laws in their mind and write them on their hearts; and I will be their God, and they shall be My people. None of them shall teach his neighbor, and none his brother, saying, 'Know the LORD,' for all shall know Me, from the least of them to the greatest of them. For I will be merciful to their unrighteousness, and their sins and their lawless deeds I will remember no more."*
>
> *In that He says, "A new covenant," He has made the first obsolete. Now what is becoming obsolete and growing old is ready to vanish away.*
>
> *Christ came as High Priest of the good things to come, with the greater and more perfect tabernacle not made with hands, that is, not of this creation. Not with the blood of goats and calves, but with His own blood He entered the Most Holy Place, once for all, having obtained eternal redemption. . . . And for this reason He is the Mediator of the new covenant, by means of death, for the redemption of the transgressions under the first covenant, that those who are called may receive the promise of the eternal inheritance. . . .*
>
> *This Man, after He had offered one sacrifice for sins forever, sat down at the right hand of God, from that time waiting till His enemies are made His footstool. For by one offering He has perfected forever those who are being sanctified (Heb. 7:22; 8:7–13; 9:11–12,15; 10:12–14).*

In order to fully understand this passage about a new covenant—the one under which we live in Christ Jesus—we must first understand what the word *covenant* means. A covenant is not a simple agreement entered into by two mutually agreeable people with the condition that if one breaks the agreement, the agreement becomes void. The Greek word for such an agreement is *suntheke*, and it is used for marriage agreements and other bonds, as well as agreement between groups of people. The Greek word in this passage is *diatheke*. It is more than an agreement; it is a *will*. The covenants God makes are agreements that God initiates; they are an act embodying His perfect will for His creation.

Because God is perfect, God alone is fully capable of keeping and upholding His covenants. Man cannot argue the terms of the covenant, only accept or reject the offer God makes. Furthermore, the covenant is not dissolved because a person rejects God's offer. God remains faithful to His offer and does not change the terms. Finally, a covenant of God always extends beyond death: it is everlasting and flows from one generation to the next. Only God can change the covenants He offers to mankind, and as presented in Scripture, God only changes covenants from good to better to best.

God initiated covenant agreements with Noah and with Abraham, but the covenant that most of the Jews knew best was the covenant God had established with the people of Israel after giving them the law through Moses. God offered the Israelites a unique relationship with Himself, but that relationship was entirely focused on their obedience to Him and their keeping of a law that had been written, according to Exodus, by God's finger of fire on tablets of stone (Ex. 31:18). The new covenant in Christ Jesus was written on the human heart.

All of God's covenants in the Bible are sealed with blood sacrifice, and this was certainly true in the covenant of the law. The consequences associated with the sins of individuals and of the nation as a whole were rolled back through blood sacrifice. Blood sacrifice did not absolve sins under the law; it only rolled back God's wrath and extended God's mercy, so a sinner might repent and amend former sinful ways and live in a way that reflected obedience to God's laws.

The new covenant established by Jesus was not an updated version of the old, but a covenant that was different in quality and in kind. The new covenant:

- was made available to the whole world. It was not limited to the Jews.

- allowed for true absolution of sin—a total forgiveness of sin.

- was linked to the granting of eternal life, not just a better life on this earth.

- prompted a fundamental change of hearts and minds. It was a covenant that would be written on the soul of man so that man would *want* to obey God out of love for Him. The keeping of the new covenant was not rooted in compulsion, but in heartfelt desire.

• was based upon a blood sacrifice that never needed to be repeated. Jesus shed His blood on the cross, once and for all. No further blood sacrifice would ever be necessary.

Pause to consider how different your relationship with God would be today had you been born three thousand years ago. Unless you are Jewish, you very likely would have believed in a pantheon of multiple gods in competition with one another, gods you would serve and attempt to bribe through gifts of food, drink, and valuable tangible tokens. None of these gods offered forgiveness to you, only sporadic peaceful coexistence with themselves and fairly unreliable but periodic provision and protection.

If you were Jewish, you would have been required to make periodic sacrifices for your sins and for your behaviors that rendered you unclean, but these sacrifices did not grant you genuine forgiveness for your sins. They only gave you an extended opportunity to repent and do good. You would have stood in hope every year on the Day of Atonement as the high priest entered the holiest place in the tabernacle or temple to offer a sacrifice for a roll-back of *all* the sins of your people committed during the previous year. Your hope would have been that the high priest survived his up-close encounter with the presence of God and that God would accept his sacrifice that was partially on your behalf. At all times you likely would have had some degree of inner struggle about obeying God. It would have been, after all, your obligation as a member of the people of God to live up to the demands of God.

The more you contemplate what life might have been like under the old covenant—or "Old Will" or "Old Testament"—surely the greater your desire to praise God for what He has made available to you under His new covenant!

A
Application for Today

Two eleven-year-old boys were having a conversation over their sack lunches during a hiking day at church camp. "How many times have you been saved?" one of them asked.

"Oh, about five," the other boy said.

"Yeah," the first boy said. "I think I've been saved about that many times too. Maybe four. Maybe six."

The boys sat silently for a few moments, and then the first boy asked, "When do you think it's finally going to take?"

The second boy considered the question for a moment and then replied soberly, "Probably not until after we get our driver's licenses and go to college."

"Yeah," the first boy agreed. "We've got a lot of revival meetings to attend before then."

Two older counselors overhearing these boys laughed to themselves, and then one of the counselors said, "We've got some work to do to get these boys squared away in their thinking about salvation!"

"We sure do," said the second counselor. "If they think their sin issues are going to end when they go to college, they're in for a surprise!"

These two boys had confused going to an altar and confessing their sins to God with truly being born anew in their spirits. The Bible's promise to us is that when we come to God and confess, "I am a sinner and I need your forgiveness so I can be in right relationship with You," God changes our sin nature. God makes us a new creation (John 3:3). We are transformed spiritually into a new being. While we may err and sin from time to time, our nature is no longer that of "sinner." Because of what Christ Jesus has done in us (1 Pet. 1:23), not because of what we have done, our spirits are cleansed and our place in heaven is secure.

What is your understanding of salvation?

Why is it freeing to know that your sin nature has been transformed and you are in right relationship with God?

What is the burden to those who believe they must be saved again every time they commit any act of disobedience against God's commandments?

S
Supplementary Scriptures to Consider

The writer of Hebrews addressed the issue of a testament, a statement of will that transcends death:

> For where there is a testament, there must also of necessity be the death of the testator. For a testament is in force after men are dead, since it has no power at all while the testator lives. Therefore not even the first covenant was dedicated without blood. For when Moses had spoken every precept to all the people according to the law, he took the blood of calves and goats, with water, scarlet wool, and hyssop, and sprinkled both the book itself and all the people, saying, "This is the blood of the covenant which God has commanded you." Then likewise he sprinkled with blood both the tabernacle and all the vessels of the ministry. And according to the law almost all things are

purified with blood, and without shedding of blood there is no remission" (Heb. 9:16–22).

- Read also these words about the institution of the Lord's Supper: "In the same manner He also took the cup after supper, saying, 'This cup is the new covenant in My blood. This do, as often as you drink it, in remembrance of Me.' For as often as you eat this bread and drink this cup, you proclaim the Lord's death till He comes" (1 Corinthians 11:25–26). Why is it important for us to *remember* the shed blood of Jesus?

- In what ways have we been purified by the shed blood of Jesus?

Hebrews makes it clear that Jesus' death ended the need for further blood sacrifice:

> It was necessary that the copies of the things in the heavens should be purified with these, but the heavenly things themselves with better sacrifices than these. For Christ has not entered the holy places made with hands, which are copies of the true, but into heaven itself, now to appear in the presence of God for us; not that He should offer Himself often, as the high priest enters the Most Holy Place every year with blood of another—He then would have had to suffer often since the foundation of the world; but now, once at the end of the ages, He has appeared to put away sin by the sacrifice of Himself. And as it is appointed for men to die once, but after this the

judgment, so Christ was offered once to bear the sins of many (Heb. 9:23–28).

- This passage states that the holy places in Israel's past were copies made by hands of the true holy place in heaven. The death and shed blood of Jesus, the eternal Son of God, was a sacrifice acknowledged in eternal heaven as being for all eternity. Reflect upon what it means for an unseen, spiritual realm to be _more real_ than the tangible, material and natural world in which we live.

- Most people living presently in the United States have never witnessed a blood sacrifice. Many people have never seen an animal slaughtered. This is not the case for many missionaries who serve Christ overseas or for those who grow up on some farms and ranches. Do you believe that our lack of experience related to the shedding of blood in any way weakens our understanding of Jesus' atoning work on the cross? Do we clearly understand the Bible truth that life is in the blood—in other words, do we have a solid understanding of the importance of blood to life? Why is this important to our acceptance of Jesus' blood being shed on our behalf?

Hebrews points to a wonderful provision made by God in His new covenant:

> But the Holy Spirit also witnesses to us; for after He had said before, "This is the covenant that I will make with them after those days, says the LORD: I will put My laws into their hearts, and in their minds I will write them," then He adds, "Their sins and their lawless deeds I will remember no more." Now where there is remission of these, there is no longer an offering for sin (Heb. 10:15–18).

• In what ways has God written His law onto your heart?

• In what ways has God written His law onto your mind?

• The good news of this passage is that once our sins have been remitted, God no longer remembers them! Therefore, we no longer need to make an offering for old sins we have confessed and for which we have received forgiveness. What are the implications of these verses to those who continually dredge up their past sins and misdeeds, asking God repeatedly to forgive them?

Hebrews notes that the new covenant gives us unprecedented access to the most holy place of God's eternal presence:

> Therefore, brethren, having boldness to enter the Holiest by the blood of Jesus, by a new and living way which He consecrated for us, through the veil, that is, His flesh, and having a High Priest over the house of God, let us draw near with a true heart in full assurance of faith, having our hearts sprinkled from an evil conscience and our bodies washed with pure water. Let us hold fast the confession of our hope without wavering, for He who promised is faithful (Heb. 10:19–23).

• Do you pray with boldness? Why or why not?

• Do you have unwavering hope that God is going to fulfill all of His promises on your behalf? Why or why not?

• Do you have an assurance that your "evil conscience" has been cleansed completely?

I
Introspection and Implications

1. A man once said, "We are saved according to God's rules, not our rules." How do you respond to that statement? Does it give you comfort, or do you feel less empowered as a person? What precisely do you perceive the rules to be regarding salvation of a sinner?

2. It has been said: "Sinners can't help but sin. Those who are saved still disobey God from time to time, but their desire is to obey, and they recognize and feel guilt for their disobedience." How do you respond to those statements? Do you sin from time to time? How do you feel? What do you do?

C
Communicating the Good News

A number of people in western cultures have very negative feelings about God's requirement of a blood sacrifice for the remission of sins. They usually say such things as, "I just don't understand why God required Jesus to die such a horrible death," or, "I like everything about Christianity except its so bloody." How do you respond to those who have such feelings and opinions?

LESSON #5

FAITH THAT OBTAINS
A GOOD TESTIMONY

*Testimony: a public profession of faith, counted
as a witness to support a claim of truth*

B
Bible Focus

Therefore do not cast away your confidence, which has
great reward. For you have need of endurance, so that after
you have done the will of God, you may receive the promise:
For yet a little while,
And He who is coming will come and will not tarry.
The just shall live by faith;
But if anyone draws back,
My soul has no pleasure in him.
But we are not of those who draw back to perdition, but of
those who believe the saving of the soul.

Now faith is the substance of things hoped for, the evidence
of things not seen. For by it the elders obtained a good
testimony.

By faith we understand that the worlds were framed by the
word of God, so that the things which are seen were not made
of things which are visible.

By faith Abel offered to God a more excellent sacrifice . . .

By faith Enoch was taken away so that he did not see
death . . .

By faith Noah, being divinely warned of things not yet seen,
moved with godly fear, prepared an ark for the saving of his
household . . .

By faith Abraham obeyed when he was called to go out to
the place which he would receive as an inheritance . . .

By faith Sarah herself also received strength to conceive
seed, and she bore a child when she was past the age, because
she judged Him faithful who had promised . . .
These all died in faith, not having received the promises, but
having seen them afar off were assured of them, embraced
them and confessed that they were strangers and pilgrims on
the earth. . . .

By faith, Abraham, when he was tested, offered up Isaac . . .

By faith Isaac blessed Jacob and Esau concerning things to
come. . . .

By faith Jacob, when he was dying, blessed each of the sons
of Joseph, and worshiped . . .

By faith Joseph, when he was dying, made mention of the
departure of the children of Israel, and gave instructions
concerning his bones. . . .

> *By faith Moses, when he became of age, refused to be*
> *called the son of Pharaoh's daughter, choosing rather to suffer*
> *affliction with the people of God than to enjoy the passing*
> *pleasures of sin. . . .*
> *By faith they passed through the Red Sea . . .*
> *By faith the walls of Jericho fell . . .*
> *By faith the harlot Rahab did not perish with those who did*
> *not believe . . .*
> *And what more shall I say? For the time would fail me to*
> *tell of Gideon and Barak and Samson and Jephthah, also of*
> *David and Samuel and the prophets: who through faith*
> *subdued kingdoms, worked righteousness, obtained promises,*
> *stopped the mouths of lions, quenched the violence of fire,*
> *escaped the edge of the sword, out of weakness were made*
> *strong, became valiant in battle, turned to flight the armies of*
> *the aliens. Women received their dead raised to life again . . .*
> *And all these, having obtained a good testimony through*
> *faith, did not receive the promise, God having provided*
> *something better for us, that they should not be made perfect*
> *apart from us (Heb. 10:35–39, 11:1-35 selected, 39–40).*

Volumes could be written on the subject of faith, and countless definitions exist for the word *faith*. But in its simplest form, faith is believing. The New Testament tells us that God gives to each person a measure of faith—in other words, an ability to believe (See Rom. 12:3). In the Christian life the starting point for using faith is believing that God exists (Heb. 11:6) and, as a close second, believing "in the saving of the soul" (Heb. 10:39), which includes believing that Jesus is the Son of God who died for our sins so that we might experience forgiveness and eternal life.

Hope and faith are vitally linked for the Christian. Hope, as described in the New Testament, is not wishful thinking. It is the future fulfillment of all things promised by God and foretold by God. Our hope is linked to some-thing tangible that is currently unseen but which is very real and reliable. What God has said will be what God accomplishes—no uncertainty or doubt about it! Our hope is certain because it is God-authored. The present mo-ment is linked with an unseen but nevertheless unbreakable chain to the future that God has already created, authorized for believers, and is unfold-ing over time.

The writer to the Hebrews declared that faith becomes the substance (the essence or reality) and the evidence (the proof or conviction) of all that the Christian hopes for in the future. In other words, a person can begin to think, speak, and act with total assurance and conviction, as if what has been promised by God is already in their possession. Presumption is *assuming* that God will act in a certain way or in a prescribed time frame, generally the way and in the timing the presumptive person desires for God to act. Genuine faith is *acting on the deepest inner conviction* that God will act in a certain way and in perfect timing because God has promised without qualification that He is going to act in that way.

The Christian believes in the reality of the spiritual realm. Furthermore, the spiritual realm precedes the natural, which means that all we know in the natural and material realm began first as a reality in the unseen spiritual realm. The word of God framed the worlds, and they became visible and continue to function as God declared.

Our forefathers in the faith, therefore, are those who acted with certainty that God had already predicted the outcome He foretold for their lives. They built an ark fully expecting rain. They stepped into the Red Sea expecting their feet to touch dry ground not water. They hid their child in a floating basket in the reeds of a river expecting their child to be rescued. The outcome in each incident briefly described in the great list of heroes of the faith in Hebrews 11 is this: those who acted by faith "obtained a good testimony"—what they believed for the short run of their lives came to pass.

The writer of Hebrews also pointed out that what these elders of the faith believed for the long-run of life has not yet *fully* come to pass, but it will! None of those on the list of overcomers saw the return of Christ Jesus and the fulfillment of all God's promises to His people. That does not make faith any less potent or effective. It simply means that part of the fulfillment of God's promises still lies ahead.

It is our believing that God is still at work in our world, unfolding and crafting His purposes toward His stated end, which gives us confidence to continue to trust in God. We can know with deep assurance that everything we speak and work by faith *will* eventually bear fruit or come to pass in perfect fulfillment. This is what it means for the just—those of us who are justified by salvation in Christ Jesus—to *live by faith.*

We must not become discouraged when we don't see immediate results. By *faith* we must see the *final* results with spiritual eyes.

What are you believing today that you don't yet see?

How do you know with deep certainty that what you are believing God to do *will* become reality?

What encouragement do you draw from the experiences of the saints of old?

A
Application for Today

"But then what did you do?" a little wide-eyed girl asked her grandmother. Grandma had been describing a camping trip she had taken with Grandpa years before. "Well, I had that small hatchet in my hand, the one I was using to chop up the dead wood from the brush where the snake was hiding out. When that snake started to coil for a strike, I picked it up by the tail and threw it on the ground and chopped it into two pieces!" Grandma said.

"Weren't you scared?" her granddaughter asked.

"Yes, in the natural I was scared," Grandma said. "But I knew I was going to get the best of that ol' snake. I just kept saying, 'I come against you in the name of Jesus, you serpent of the devil!' It never had a chance!"

Grandma noticed that her young grandson, who had been listening intently to the conversation, hadn't said a word but seemed impressed by what he had heard. Later that afternoon, she overheard a conversation between her grandson and his best friend from next door. "Yeah," said her grandson, "you may think my Grandma is old and sweet and bakes cookies and all that, but let me tell you, my Grandma is no wimp!"

Who do you know that embodies faith in action? What about their life encourages you to trust God in times of trouble?

S
Supplementary Scriptures to Consider

The writer of Hebrews said this about the way we approach God with our faith:

> But without faith it is impossible to please Him, for he who comes to God must believe that He is, and that He is a rewarder of those who diligently seek Him (Heb. 11:6).

• In what ways do you believe it is impossible to *please* God without faith? (Hint: Contrast faith with works.) To please God means to have God's approval as the result of obeying God's Word. Do you have assurance that you are *pleasing* to God? If so, why so? If not, what might you do?

- Do you believe God exists? What do you say to a person who *doesn't* believe God exists or who *isn't sure* whether God exists?

- In what ways is God a *rewarder* of those who believe? How have you been rewarded by your belief in God?

- What does it mean to you that God's rewarding is for "those who diligently seek Him"? How, in practical ways, do you seek God?

Faith is presented in Hebrews as one of the rudiments, or elementary principles, of a life in Christ Jesus:

> Leaving the discussion of the elementary principles of Christ, let us go on to perfection, not laying again the foundation of repentance from dead works and of faith toward God, of the doctrine of baptisms, of laying on of hands, of resurrection of the dead, and of eternal judgment (Heb. 6:1–2).

• What is the link in your life between "repentance from dead works" and "faith toward God"?

• Do you consider your faith to be the *foundation* for your Christian life? How so?

The apostle Paul wrote this to the Romans about faith:

> The righteousness of faith speaks in this way . . . "The word is near you, in your mouth and in your heart" (that is, the word of faith which we preach): that if you confess with your mouth the Lord Jesus and believe in your heart that God has raised Him from the dead, you will be saved. For with the heart one believes unto righteousness, and with the mouth confession is made unto salvation. For the Scripture says, "Whoever believes on Him will not be put to shame" (Rom. 10:6, 8–11).

• In what ways has confessing your faith been a demonstration of your faith?

- What is it that you confess in your testimony about Christ Jesus being your Savior? Can you confess something you don't believe? Can you believe something you don't confess? Why do you believe the apostle Paul links the two: believing and confessing?

I
Introspection and Implications

1. In what specific ways do you consider a life of faith to be a courageous life?

2. Hebrews says, "The just shall live by faith"—which is a quote from Habakkuk 2:4. What does it mean to you to *live* by faith? Do you consider yourself to be a just person who is challenged by God's Word to live this way?

3. "The faith" is a term used to describe Christianity. "Personal faith" refers to the believing power of an individual. How does your personal faith in Christ Jesus help you "keep the faith" of those who have gone before you in the faith?

4. What are you hoping today? Is your faith the substance and evidence of that hope? Do you see yourself as already having been granted what it is that you believe God will do, even if you have not yet seen the fulfillment of God's promise? Why or why not?

C
Communicating the Good News

In what ways does a sinner (non-believer) already believe certain things?

How do you explain to a person who is spiritually lost their need to accept Jesus as their Savior *by faith*?

How do you explain the phrase to "put your faith in Christ Jesus" to an unbeliever? What action steps would you encourage the person to take?

LESSON #6

RUNNING THE FAITH RACE

Weight: a heavy load or burden

B
Bible Focus

> *Therefore we also, since we are surrounded by so great a*
> *cloud of witnesses, let us lay aside every weight, and the sin*
> *which so easily ensnares us, and let us run with endurance the*
> *race that is set before us, looking unto Jesus, the author and*
> *finisher of our faith, who for the joy that was set before Him*
> *endured the cross, despising the shame, and has sat down at*
> *the right hand of the throne of God (Heb. 12:1–2).*

Few passages of the New Testament have so much spiritual meaning packed into so few words! Consider the wealth of instruction and encouragement in these seven phrases:

- *The race that is set before us*. Each of us has a faith race to run. The fact of the race is a certainty for all believers. The goal of the race is the fullness of life in Christ Jesus, which is ultimately heaven. The race is different for each person when it comes to the context of the race, the time, place, and circumstances surrounding the race.

How do you describe this race in *your* life?

- *Looking unto Jesus, the author and finisher of our faith*. Jesus is our goal but also our way to the goal. He is the supreme example of a life lived fully by faith. Jesus gave us our faith when we were created as human being and also as a spiritually renewed believer. Jesus was and is the Word at the creation of all things, including every individual person. He was and is the Word at the creation of every new spiritual being. He is the One who is the author of our salvation. It is equally true that Jesus is the finisher of all things pertaining to spiritual perfection. It is Jesus who enables us to put an end to sin and to embrace the wholeness God offers to us.

In what areas of your life do you look to Jesus continually?
In what ways do you consider Jesus to be the author of your faith?
In what ways do you rely upon Jesus to be the finisher of your faith?

- The joy that was set before Him. Jesus ran the earthly race of His life with joy. We are to follow His example! Even in the face of the pain and shame of the cross, Jesus ran His race joyfully, believing for the full rewards of gaining the souls of believing mankind and being seated at the right hand of the throne of God.

What gives you joy as you run your faith race?

What rewards are you trusting God to give you as you endure the hardships of this life?

- *Surrounded by so great a cloud of witnesses.* Those who have been the heroes of faithfulness are to inspire us. This phrase does not mean that believers from the past are heavenly spectators observing our conduct but rather that we are to draw encouragement from those who have given testimony by the examples of their lives.

Who has inspired you by their faith-based experiences to trust in God and manifest *your* faith in a difficult or challenging time or circumstance?

- *Lay aside every weight.* Weights are hindrances to running. What slows us down or holds us back from moving forward in our faith? The weights of doubt and fear. We must lay these aside, acknowledging them but refusing to allow them to influence actions that we know God desires us to take.

In what ways are you laying aside every weight today?

- *Lay aside . . . the sin which so easily ensnares us.* Every person has to battle with sin, even though he or she has been transformed into a new spiritual creature. We still live in human bodies and have not-yet-fully-renewed minds that present us with temptations. Hebrews tells us these areas of potential sin in our lives are like traps. We must be aware of them so we can sidestep them or leap over them any time the devil attempts to trip us.

Are you aware of your areas of weakness? What are you doing to avoid temptation in those areas?

- *Run with endurance.* We are to run with endurance—lasting, persevering power. If we fall, we get up. If we fail, we ask for God's forgiveness, make amends with others, forgive ourselves, and move forward. If we are momentarily delayed, we reactivate our will to do what we know God is calling us to do. If we become weak, we renew our commitment to excel in Christ Jesus. We are not in a sprint to the finish line but rather, a marathon.

How are you developing endurance in your faith? What is God using to develop persevering power in you? In what ways are you relying upon the Holy Spirit for endurance in your relationship with Christ Jesus?

A
Application for Today

"Watcha doing, Dad?" a little boy asked as he watched his father rummage through the upper shelf of a closet.

"Looking for a pair of old running shoes."

"Why?" the boy asked.

"Because I'm going to go out for a little run."

"Why?" the boy asked again as his father found the shoes and began to lace them on. The father grinned. "Why" was one of his son's favorite questions.

"Because I got on the scales this morning and took a long look at myself in the mirror and said, 'Dad, you are out of shape! It's time to start exercising again!'"

The boy looked at his father with squinted eyes and then concluded, "Your shape looks alright to me."

"Thanks," Dad said, "but *round* is not the shape I want for my stomach!"

"How'd you get out of shape?" the boy asked.

"I stopped doing what I knew I needed to do," Dad said. "I started eating too much and running too little."

"Oh," said the boy. "How long do you have to run?"

"Today," Dad said, "about fifteen minutes. But it's more important that I run or walk several days a week, for the rest of my life."

"Run for the rest of your life?" the boy asked in amazement. "That's a lot of running."

"Right! That's a lot of running, but I want to do a lot of living," Dad replied. "There are lots of things ahead I still want to do with you. And someday when you are just a little bit older, we'll get you a pair of running shoes so you can run with me!"

Nobody gets out of shape spiritually or physically in a day. It's the disciplines of our lives that keep us in shape for the great race we are challenged to run with our faith. Nobody builds discipline into another person's daily schedule. We each must do it ourselves.

What daily disciplines have you built into your life to give you endurance for the long haul when it comes to your faith race?

S
Supplementary Scriptures to Consider

The writer to the Hebrews gave this advice about renewing spiritual vitality, a necessity for faith that endures:

> Strengthen the hands which hang down, and the feeble knees,
> and make straight paths for your feet, so that what is lame
> may not be dislocated, but rather be healed (Heb. 12: 12–13).

- To have "hands which hang down" is a reference not only to prayer, but to warfare. The Jewish stance of prayer is standing, with hands raised from the elbows. The person with hands hanging down is a person who has stopped praying. The warrior with hands hanging down is a warrior who has become so weary in wielding his sword or lifting his shield that he becomes vulnerable in battle. Reflect on the ways in which prayer is linked to the winning of spiritual battles. Do you have "hands which hang down" in your prayer life? How might you strengthen your prayer life?

- Feeble knees are knees that keep a person from standing and walking with agility, speed, or sure footing. Repeatedly throughout His Word, God calls upon His people to *stand*. People tend to faint or fall because they allow fears and worries to overwhelm them. The opposite of fear is faith. Do you have spiritually feeble knees today? What might you do to strengthen your faith and overcome the fears and anxieties that keep you from living with strength?

- To make straight your paths is to remove everything contrary to a life in Christ Jesus from your daily routines. Are your paths straight today? How might you make them straight?

- The purpose for our strengthening our prayer life and faith and for removing all spiritual obstacles from our race toward perfection in Christ Jesus is this: so the areas of weakness in our lives (lameness) might be healed. The alternative is for our weaknesses to continue to the point that we are severely disabled spiritually (described as dislocation in this passage). Are there areas of your life that are in danger of becoming permanently disabled? What might you do?

The statement in Hebrews 12:12–13 is likely drawn from the passage below from the Old Testament:

> Strengthen the weak hands,
> And make firm the feeble knees.
> Say to those who are fearful-hearted,
> "Be strong, do not fear!
> Behold, your God will come with vengeance,
> With the recompense of God;
> He will come and save you."
> Then the eyes of the blind shall be opened,
> And the ears of the deaf shall be unstopped.
> Then the lame shall leap like a deer,
> And the tongue of the dumb sing . . .

A highway shall be there, and a road,
And it shall be called the Highway of Holiness.
The unclean shall not pass over it . . .
But the redeemed shall walk there,
And the ransomed of the Lord shall return,
And come to Zion with singing,
With everlasting joy on their heads.
They shall obtain joy and gladness,
And sorrow and sighing shall flee away
(Is. 35:3–6, 8–10).

• What stands out in a special way to you in this passage from Isaiah?

• In what practical ways do you speak to yourself, "Be strong, do not fear"?

• In what ways do you speak to others, "Be strong, do not fear"?

The apostle Paul also spoke in terms of a spiritual race toward the fullness of all that God has designed as one's purpose in life:

> Not that I have already attained, or am already perfected; but I press on, that I may lay hold of that for which Christ Jesus has also laid hold of me. Brethren, I do not count myself to have apprehended; but one thing I do, forgetting those things which are behind and reaching forward to those things which are ahead, I press toward the goal for the prize of the upward call of God in Christ Jesus (Phil. 3:12–14).

• Why is it important to the running of your faith race that you leave the past behind you? In what ways is this related to receiving God's forgiveness, forgiving others, and forgiving yourself?

• How do you define the "the prize of the upward call of God in Christ Jesus"? What specifically does this prize include for you personally?

The book of Proverbs links wisdom to walking a straight and right path:

> I have taught you in the way of wisdom;
> I have led you in right paths.
> When you walk, your steps will not be hindered,
> And when you run, you will not stumble.
> Take firm hold of instruction, do not let go;
> Keep her, for she is your life (Prov. 4:11–13).

• In what areas of weakness are you seeking instruction?

• How might greater instruction, including greater insight into the Word of God, help you make your path straight as you run your faith race?

I

Introspection and Implications

1. What rewards do you believe lie at the end of your race? Are all of these rewards in eternity, or do you believe some of them are ones you can, should, or will experience in this life?

2. In what ways is a race *unlike* a stroll? Identify several differences. What does this metaphor of a race mean to you in your spiritual faith race?

3. At no time are we told that our spiritual faith race is a race against another person or group of people. At the same time we are told that we are in a *race*, not a personal jog through the park. Who or what are we running against?

C
Communicating the Good News

Faith is not passive. It is active. The simple act of believing is all that a person needs for receiving Christ Jesus into their life as Savior, but believing even in this case, is not passive. A person must *choose* to believe with their will. How do you express this to an unbeliever?

LESSON #7

BECOMING COMPLETE

*Complete: having every necessary part or everything
that is wanted; to make something whole*

B
Bible Focus

> *Now may the God of peace who brought up our Lord Jesus*
> *from the dead, that great Shepherd of the sheep, through the*
> *blood of the everlasting covenant, make you complete in every*
> *good work to do His will, working in you what is well pleas-*
> *ing in His sight, through Jesus Christ, to whom be glory*
> *forever and ever. Amen. (Hebrews 13:20–21)*

Countless Christians around the world long to be "blessed" by God. They often define God's blessing in terms of healing and health, joy, material increase, enhanced family relationships, spiritual gifts, and in other ways. God's Word tells us that Christians *are* blessed, but it also states that we are not to aspire to blessing as much as we are to seek to be *whole*. We are to long for completion, which includes spiritual maturity, deep trust in God, and a fullness of God's power and provision, so we might fulfill God's plan and purpose for us on this earth. We are to long for God's *well-pleasing* approval of all things that we think, say, and do. The closing of the book of Hebrews underscores this.

Note, however, that we cannot make ourselves complete. Our work does not qualify us for completion. Neither are we capable in ourselves of doing "every good work." Hebrews states that our wholeness or completion is the work of the Great Shepherd, as part of His everlasting covenant with us. It is Christ Jesus who brings us to fulfillment and perfection. It is God who uses our work to complete His plans and accomplish His purposes, and thus, it is God who completes our work.

What is our part in this process? Elsewhere in the book of Hebrews we find three specific things we are to do that put us into position for the Great Shepherd to do His work in us.

First, we are challenged to read and heed the Word of God:

> Let us therefore be diligent to enter that rest, lest anyone fall
> according to the same example of disobedience. For the word of
> God is living and powerful, and sharper than any two-edged sword,
> piercing even to the division of soul and spirit, and of joints and
> marrow, and is a discerner of the thoughts and intents of the heart.
> And there is no creature hidden from His sight, but all things are
> naked and open to the eyes of Him to whom we must give account
> (Heb. 4:11–13).

The Word of God renews our minds and convicts us of changes we need to make in our lives. This renewal power is part of the way God moves us from fragmentation to completion, from weakness to strength, from immaturity to maturity. It is as we read and apply the truth of God's Word to our lives that our faith is strengthened, and we see more clearly how the Holy Spirit desires to work in us and through us.

Second, when we are chastened by the Lord, we are to seek God's purpose for our chastening and to yield to God's will, learning the lessons He desires us to learn.

> If you endure chastening, God deals with you as with sons; for what son is there whom a father does not chasten? . . . Now no chastening seems to be joyful for the present, but painful; nevertheless, afterward it yields the peaceable fruit of righteousness to those who have been trained by it (Heb. 12:7,11).

God is quick to convict us, by the power of His Holy Spirit working in us, when we err or stray from His path of obedience. When we face difficult times in our lives, we must recognize that God is at work. He will use all things in our lives to bring us to the very center of His will for us. Our first questions must be, "What am I to learn from this? How am I to change? What is God seeking to do in me or through me?"

The chastening of the Lord is never a condemning or purposeless punishment, although what we experience may be temporarily painful. God chastens us to perfect us and to train us for even greater purpose and rewards. He uses even hard times to bring us to greater wholeness.

Third, we are to refrain from exploring false doctrines and religions. We are to look to the unchanging nature of Christ Jesus as our example of unwavering steadfastness.

> Jesus Christ is the same yesterday, today, and forever. Do not be carried about with various and strange doctrines. For it is good that the heart be established by grace, not with foods which have not profited those who have been occupied with them (Heb. 13:8–9).

Those who wander willfully into false doctrines and false religions delay their own completion. Their detour into error will result in chastening. Only those who seek to be "established by grace" are in the right position to be made whole.

Do you have a strong sense that you are you being made complete in Christ today? To what do you point as evidence?

Are you diligently reading and applying God's Word, looking only to Christ as your source of spiritual renewal and strength?

Are you experiencing chastening from the Lord? Are you learning lessons from the difficult or challenging time you may be experiencing?

A
Application for Today

"Why did this happen to me?" the young woman cried. "I've lost every-thing!"

Her spiritual mentor replied, "No, you haven't lost everything."

"Yes, I have!" the woman continued to cry.

"No!" the mentor said more sternly. "You have not lost Christ Jesus."

The woman quieted.

"The best question to ask is not *why*," the mentor continued. "The question to ask at this point is this: 'What *now*, Lord?'"

Any time a person experiences a deep sense of loss or lack, the first question the person is likely to ask is "why?" Seldom, however, does God tell us why. Rather, God has promised to lead us *and accompany us* into our future no matter what happens to us. We are to trust Him even without why explanations.

We can count on God's presence with us. He does not leave us nor forsake us at any time. Furthermore, no tragedy, failure, or loss takes God by surprise. He always has a plan for us to move closer to our completion of purpose, to our development of the character perfection of Christ Jesus, and to all of the eternal rewards He has prepared for us. God not only desires for us to be whole, but He has a plan for making us whole that is never derailed by earthly circumstances.

Recall a time of loss or lack in your life. What did you do? What did God do? What is God *still* doing?

S
Supplementary Scriptures to Consider

The writer of Hebrews described a role that a church has in helping a person be in the best possible position for God to do His sovereign work:

> And let us consider one another in order to stir up love and good works, not forsaking the assembling of ourselves to-gether, as is the manner of some, but exhorting one another, and so much the more as you see the Day approaching (Heb. 10:24–25).

• How do you help another person to "stir up love and good works"? Do you allow others to help you in this way?

• Have you ever avoided going to church or getting involved in a church fully? What is the danger of "forsaking the assembling"?

• Exhorting is generally a matter of declaring what is right and wrong. Are you reluctant when it comes to exhorting others? If so, why? If not, why not?

Do you have a negative reaction toward the idea of being exhorted by others? If so, why?

The writer of Hebrews had this to say about the importance of living a godly life in one's relationship with other people:

> Pursue peace with all people, and holiness, without which no one will see the Lord: looking carefully lest anyone fall short of the grace of God; lest any root of bitterness springing up cause trouble, and by this many become defiled (Heb. 12:14–15).

• What does it mean to you to pursue peace?

• What does it mean to you to pursue holiness?

- Peaceful relationships with other believers and holiness are held out in this passage as prerequisites for seeing God at work in the midst of a church. Can you cite an example of this being true in your experience as a church member?

- To what extent do you feel responsible that other people in your church do not "fall short of the grace of God"—in other words, fail to receive all that God has for them spiritually?

- How does bitterness develop between people or among factions in a church?

What types of trouble does bitterness cause? In what way does bitterness defile a group of believers?

The writer of Hebrews placed emphasis on brotherly love, entertaining strangers, and remembering prisoners:

> Let brotherly love continue. Do not forget to entertain strangers, for by so doing some have unwittingly entertained angels. Remember the prisoners as if chained with them—those who are mistreated—since you yourselves are in the body also (Heb. 13:1–3).

• In what ways do you find it difficult at times to "let brotherly love continue"?

• Have you ever entertained a stranger and wondered later if that stranger had been an angel? What happened?

• What is our responsibility toward prisoners around the world who are in confinement, and often torment, for their faith?

The writer of Hebrews identified three attributes for believers to seek and embody:

1. *Contentment.* Let your conduct be without covetousness; be content with such things as you have (Heb. 13:5).

2. *Generosity.* Do not forget to do good and to share, for with such sacrifices God is well pleased (Heb.13:16).

3. *Submissiveness to authority.* Obey those who rule over you, and be submissive, for they watch out for your souls, as those who must give account. Let them do so with joy and not with grief, for that would be unprofitable for you (Heb. 13:17).

• How do you respond to each of these statements? Do they cause any feelings of conviction in you? What might you do?

- How do each of these attributes relate to our becoming more whole or complete?

I
Introspection and Implications

What is the balance between a believer trusting the Great Shepherd for completion and that believer actively seeking to do the right thing and be the best person possible? In other words, what is the balance between doing your part and trusting God to do His part in bringing you to wholeness? How do you strike that balance in your life?

C
Communicating the Good News

What is it that you hold out to an unsaved person as the work God promises to do in that person's life after he or she accepts Jesus as Savior? On what basis do you believe God desires to do that work and *will* do that work? Do you place conditions on either the desire of God or the work of God in bringing a new believer to wholeness?

NOTES TO LEADERS
OF SMALL GROUPS

As the leader of a small discussion group, think of yourself as a facilitator with three main roles:

- Get the discussion started

- Involve every person in the group

- Encourage an open, candid discussion that remains Bible-focused

You certainly don't need to be the person with all the answers! In truth, much of your role is to be a person who asks questions:

- What really impacted you most in this lesson?

- Was there a particular part of the lesson or a question that you found troubling?

- Was there a particular part of the lesson that you found encouraging or insightful?

- Was there a particular part of the lesson that you'd like to explore further?

Express to the group at the outset of your study that your goal as a group is to gain new insights into God's Word; this is not the forum for defending a point of doctrine or a theological opinion. Stay focused on what God's Word says and means. The purpose of the study is also to share insights on how to apply God's Word to everyday life. *Every* person in the group can and should contribute. The collective wisdom that flows from Bible-focused discussion is often very rich and deep.

Seek to create an environment in which every member of the group feels free to ask questions of other members in order to gain greater understanding. Encourage the group members to voice their appreciation to one another for new insights gained and to be supportive of one another personally. Take the lead in doing this. Genuinely appreciate and value the contributions made by each person.

You may want to begin each study by having one or more members of the group read through the section provided under "Bible Focus." Ask the group specifically if it desires to discuss any of the questions under the "Application" section, the "Supplemental Scriptures" section, and the "Implications" and "Communicating the Gospel" sections. You do not need to bring closure—or come to a definitive conclusion or consensus—about any one question asked in this study. Rather, if the group does not *have* a satisfactory Bible-based answer to a question, encourage them to engage in further "asking, seeking, and knocking" strategies to discover the answers! Remember the words of Jesus: "Ask, and it will be given to you, seek, and you will find; knock, and it will be opened to you. For everyone who asks receives, and he who seeks finds, and to him who knocks it will be opened" (Matt. 7:7–8).

Finally, open and close your study with prayer. Ask the Holy Spirit, whom Jesus called the Spirit of Truth, to guide your discussion and to reveal what is of eternal benefit to you individually and as a group. As you close your study, ask the Holy Spirit to seal to your remembrance what you have read and studied and to show you in the upcoming days, weeks, and months *ways* to apply what you have studied to your daily life and relationships.

General Themes for the Lessons

Each lesson in this study has one or more core themes. Continually pull the group back to these themes. You can do this by asking simple questions, such as, "How is that related to _____?" or "How does that help us better understand the concept of _____?" or "In what ways does that help us apply the principle of _____?"

A summary of general themes or concepts in each lesson is provided below:

Lesson #1
JESUS, THE HEIR OF ALL THINGS
The inheritance of Jesus
Our being joint heirs with Jesus
What God desires to create in us

Lesson #2

JESUS, OUR SUFFERING SAVIOR

Propitiation for sin

Power of death: fear of suffering

Fear of death: no eternity

The lessons and benefits associated with suffering

Lesson #3

JESUS, OUR HIGH PRIEST FOREVER

The role of having a high priest (for Christians living today)

Jesus' pursuit of lost souls

Lesson #4

JESUS, SURETY OF A BETTER COVENANT

God's covenant with us

Forgiveness of a sinner

Forgiveness of sins

Blood sacrifice

Lesson #5

FAITH THAT OBTAINS A GOOD TESTIMONY

The relationship between faith and hope

Faith versus presumption

The rewards for those who have faith—now and in the future

Living by faith

Lesson #6

RUNNING THE FAITH RACE

Ways in which our faith races are similar and unique

The spiritual disciplines necessary for a successful faith race

Lesson #7

BECOMING COMPLETE

Wholeness

Chastening versus punishment

The role of other believers in our becoming whole or complete as individual Christians

NOTES

NOTES

NOTES